P9-AER-533

SHORT, GREEN AND HANDSOME

Copyright © 1984 by Henson Associates, Inc.

The MUPPET Show, MUPPETS and MUPPET character names are trademarks of Henson Associates, Inc.

The MUPPET comic strips are distributed world wide by King Features Syndicate, Inc.

A TOR Book

Published by Tom Doherty Associates, 8-10 West 36 Street, New York, New York 10018

First TOR printing: July 1984

ISBN: 0-812-57363-3

Printed in the United States of America

Jim Henson's
MUPPETS

By
Guy & Brad Gilchrist

SHORT, GREEN
AND HANDSOME

TOR

A TOM DOHERTY ASSOCIATES BOOK

TO LAUREN AND
GARRETT ♡

Dear Miss Piggy

Dear Miss P., I had a terrible accident at a Dinner Party last night.

What's best for getting gravy stains out of Silk? (SIGNED) SPOTTY

Dear Spotty, THE MAID.

TIKA TIKA TIK

KERMIE...WOULD YOU LIKE TO GO OUT WITH ME THIS EVENING?

WELL, PIGGY... LET ME SAY THIS ABOUT THAT: AS MUCH AS THE PARTY OF THE FIRST PART WOULD ENJOY BEING ABLE TO ADVISE THE PARTY OF THE SECOND PART IN REFERENCE TO SAID P.M. IN A POS... FASHION, I AM AFRAID THAT FOR HITHERT... REASONS OF NATIONAL SECURITY I MUST... SURRENDER ALL RIGHTS TO PRO CHANNE... SAID PRIOR ENGAGEMENT, IPSOF THER... CERTAIN ALIENABLE RIGHTS IN... QUIRY TO SAID PROCESSES REAS... CONTRAR... FACTORS IN APP LICA... TO, WITH, ON, OR OUT INTER LESS... NINETY DAYS WITHOU

ZZZZ

WORKS EVERY TIME!

GUY& BRAD GILGORE

2-9

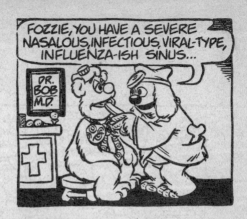

Dear Miss Piggy

Dear Miss P: I'm used to cooking for a BIG family, but now the kids are grown up.

What's the best way to use Leftovers?
SIGNED Still Cooking

Dear STILL: What's a LEFTOVER?

TIKA TIKA TIK

HEY, CHEF! THIS STUFF IS PRETTY TASTY!!

ËRF YU LIJKË DËR DĬRŚCHY DĬRŚCHY, YU VUN LØØPY DËR VØN ZØØPY ZØØPY!!

ER- WHAT DID HE SAY?

HE SAID, "IF YOU LIKED THE DISH-WATER, WAIT'LL YOU TRY MY SOUP!"

GUY & BRAD GILCHRIST 1-23

Dear Miss P: We've been invited to the "Gala White House Lawn Party."

What can we do to show our deepest Appreciation? (SIGNED) In With The In Crowd.

Dear In: EASY! Send MOI your tickets!!

GUY & BRAD GILCHRIST

TIKA TIKA TIK!

1-5

WHY DON'T YOU WATCH WHERE YOU'RE GOIN', BO?!

THAT'S WHAT I WAS DOING!

6-3

WELL, GONZO... YOU'VE HIKED ALL THE WAY UP TO "PARACHUTE POINT"!

IT'S TIME TO CAST OFF THE DOUBTS AND FEARS AND... *GO FOR IT!*

GERONIMO!!

ACTUALLY, IT WAS TIME TO CAST OFF THE BACKPACK, AND PUT ON A PARACHUTE....

11-30

Dear Miss P: I'm in love with a PILOT who's a real hunk! But... I'm just an ugly duckling!

Should I try for this HIGHFLYER, or just stay GROUNDED?
—— DUCKLING

GUY & BRAD GILCHRIST

Dear Duck: Forget him! It's no use trying for FIRST CLASS with an EXCURSION-FARE FACE!

TIKA TIKA TIK!

5-B

9-21

5-5

4-16

HUMPTY DUMPTY SAT ON A WALL. HUMPTY DUMPTY HAD A GREAT FALL.

UNCLE RIZZO'S RHYMES

HE JUST HAD TO LAY THERE, AFTER THIS SAD OCCURRENCE...

FOR POOR HUMPTY HAD NO MEDICAL INSURANCE.

6-2

ONE THING ALL RUNNERS HATE IS THE SOUND OF ANOTHER RUNNER GAINING ON THEM!

CLOP
CLOP
CLOP

CLOP
CLOP
CLOP

GUY & BRAD GILCHRIST

CLOP!
CLOP!

9-5

6-18

12-5